THE ANSONIA

A Pictorial History of Manhattan's Beaux-Arts Masterpiece

Written & Designed
by

Copyright 2015
by The Cardinals

All Rights Reserved. No part of this publication may be reproduced, stored in a retrieval system, or transmitted in any form or by any means, electronic, email, photocopying, recording, scanning, or otherwise, without the prior written permission of the Publisher. The content of this book is of a historical, educational, and newsworthy nature, and is made available in the name of the public interest. Considering the purpose and character of the transformative use of the text and photos in creating a new work, the Publisher is confident that their use does not directly affect and/ or compete with any potential claimant's business or potential for income. The Publishers are confident that there is no part of this book that is in violation of, or infringes upon, anyone's copyrights, trademarks, licensing, privacy, or postmortem publicity rights.

Limit of Liability/Disclaimer of Warranty: While the Publishers and the Author(s) have used their best efforts in preparing this book, they make no representations or warranties with respect to the accuracy or completeness of the contents of this book and specifically disclaim any implied warranties of merchantability or fitness for a particular purpose. Neither the Publisher nor the Author(s) shall be liable for any loss of profit or any other commercial damages, including, but not limited to, special, incidental, consequential, or other damages.

All reasonable effort has been made to contact the photographers and copyright owners of all images printed in this publication. Any omissions or errors are inadvertent and will be corrected in subsequent editions, provided written notification is sent to the Publisher. Many of the images in this book are transformative works and are protected by their own copyrights as well as the overall copyright protecting the contents of this book.

The Campfire Network publishes its books in a variety of formats. Some content that appears in print may not be available in electronic books, and vice versa. The content of this book was generated during scholarly research on architectural history.

For information on any books published by the Campfire Network, or for bulk & wholesale orders, or to schedule interviews with any of the Authors, please contact Cardinal@CampfireNetwork.com.

Acknowledgments & Dedication

It affords us great and sincere pleasure to acknowledge and dedicate this book to Catherine and Robert Harper in appreciation of their deep and active interest in the history of the Ansonia, and for the unbounded enthusiasm they have expressed in our research. In addition, their tireless, generous and remarkably keen feedback deserve the highest praise and appreciation that can be expressed.

We also want to express our sincere gratitude to Joe Franklin, Neil McEachern, Jack Perry, Steve Silberberg, and D.C. Blackbird for their time, talent, friendship, and feedback. A special thanks goes to Mr. Andrew Alpern for his many useful observations, which can not be too highly emphasized, and for being the inspiration for the serious study of various aspects of architectural history.

Despite all the contributions made from so many people, from so many sources, the responsibility for any errors, omissions, misinterpretations, or shortcomings anywhere in this book remain ours alone.

For
Bridgette, Jekyll, Autumn and Double-Stuff.

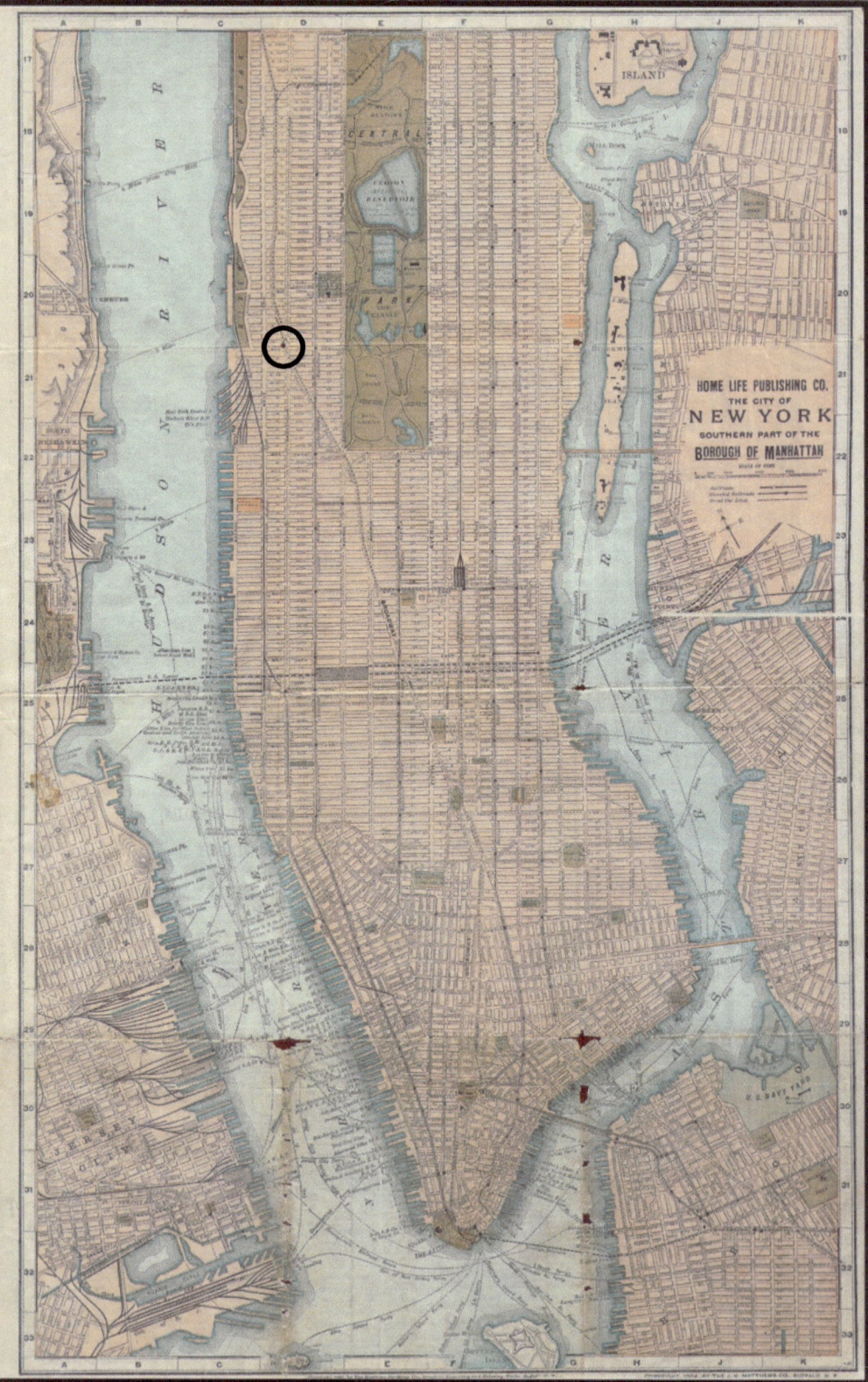

Contents

Introduction

Chapter 1:   Illustrations
Chapter 2:   Ads & Articles
Chapter 3:   Postcards
Chapter 4:   Construction
Chapter 5:   View from Roof
Chapter 6:   Floor Plans
Chapter 7:   Restaurants
Chapter 8:   Menus
Chapter 9:   Lobby
Chapter 10: Assembly Room
Chapter 11: A Glimpse Inside
Chapter 12: W.E.D. Stokes
Chapter 13: Residents
Chapter 14: View from Broadway

A PICTORIAL HISTORY

THE ANSONIA

Introduction

THE ANSONIA: IMAGES & MEMORIES is a collection of vintage and rare images with accompanying captions and information that tell the visual story of the early history of the Ansonia, from the time William Earle Dodge Stokes began purchasing the land on New York's Upper West Side, through construction, its grand opening in 1904, and the first several decades that followed. Carefully selected images offer a unique glimpse of the extraordinary building that was once the largest hotel in the world and is now one of New York's most beautiful residential buildings.

A PICTORIAL HISTORY

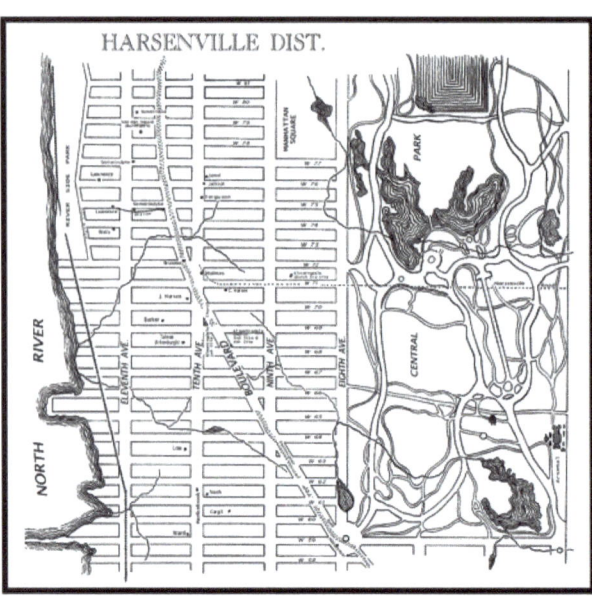

During the 1700s and 1800s the area between 58th - 81st Streets was known as Harsenville. The district took its name from Jacob Harson whose father-in-law purchased the land in 1701. By the time the Ansonia was constructed, the name "Harsenville" had long since been out of use and the area was simply known as the Upper West Side.

Plate 6, Part of Section 4: [Bounded by W. 77th Street, Amsterdam Avenue, W. 71st Street, West End Avenue, W. 72nd Street]. 1898-1899. Atlas of the City of New York, Borough of Manhattan. From Actual Surveys and Official Plans.

THE ANSONIA

One

ILLUSTRATIONS

An architectural rendering of the east elevation showing the central tower as it was intended to look. Ultimately, only the base of the tower was built.

A PICTORIAL HISTORY

1909 Illustration of the Ansonia by American artist & author Joseph Pennell (1857 –1926).

THE ANSONIA

New York Tribune, 1902.

A PICTORIAL HISTORY

Sketch of 72nd Street between Amsterdam Avenue and Broadway, circa 1900.

Two

Ads & Articles

THE FLAT-DWELLERS OF A GREAT CITY

THE TYPICAL EXPERIENCE OF PEOPLE WHO LIVE IN THE BIG NEW YORK APARTMENT BUILDINGS—THE ENORMOUS GROWTH OF APARTMENT-HOUSES — HOW THEY CONTRIBUTE TO THE INDIVIDUAL LIFE AND THAT OF THE COMMUNITY

BY

ALBERT BIGELOW PAINE

(Illustrated from photographs taken by the author)

A SHORT time ago the tenement dweller—a person whose habitation was bounded on the top and bottom by other habitations, and who sometimes found it cheaper to move than to pay rent—was scorned by the house-dweller, who had upstairs, downstairs and basement, secured for a term of years. Today it is said that nine-tenths of the population of Manhattan Island are dwellers in tenements, and that one-half of them move from one to six times yearly. I have heard of a family that moved three times in one month.

The word "tenement" is no longer popular. We hear of "flats" and "apartments" now, of rentals as high as $6,000 and even $10,000 a year, but the law makes no distinction. Every house, however big and expensive, which contains layers of inhabitants, all duly recorded, labeled and pigeonholed, is a "tenement."

The rise and progress of the New York City "flat-dweller" presents a sociological object lesson. It begins, as likely as not, with a young man from the country. He has secured employment in the metropolis at wages which seem liberal, and with good prospect of advancement. Almost immediately he begins to plan for a home. He cannot afford a house. The Sunday papers

THE ANSONIA
The largest apartment house in New York city

Photographed by Irving Underhill

A PICTORIAL HISTORY

14

Ad placed in the San Francisco Chronicle on February 1, 1901.

Ad placed in the New York Daily Tribune. September 20, 1903.

THE ANSONIA

1926 Ad to publicize the Ansonia's rooms.

The Washington Times. April 28, 1918. Text: Ansonia Hotel, at Seventy-Third Street and Broadway, which imperial Germany's murderers plotted to destroy during a ball at which all the navigating officers of the Atlantic squadron would be present. The conspiracy was foiled by the United States Secret Service.

A PICTORIAL HISTORY

THE ANSONIA

Photo of the southeast corner of the Ansonia that accompanied a 1907 article in the American Architect.

Advertisement in The Official Hotel Red Book and Directory, 1917.

THE ANSONIA

Three

POSTCARDS

Mass produced souvenir postcards of city scenes and landmarks such as this one were wildly popular between the years 1898 - 1918 which was considered to be the "Golden Age of Postcards." Though the United States had the largest consumer market, many of the postcards were imported from European countries whose engravers and colorists may never have seen the actual places depicted. This explains the artistic license used when colorizing the buildings and scenes in some postcards.

Southeast corner of the Ansonia with a view of the monument to opera composer Giuseppe Verdi, erected in 1906, in the foreground.

Close-up of the monument to opera composer Giuseppe Verdi, erected in 1906. The statue was designed by Pasquale Civiletti (1858–1952). Statues of four of his most famous characters (Falstaff, Leonora of La forza del destino, Aida and Otello) are on the base below him. Flowers around the statue bloom in the spring and summer months.

A PICTORIAL HISTORY

THE ANSONIA

A PICTORIAL HISTORY

THE ANSONIA

A PICTORIAL HISTORY

THE ANSONIA

A PICTORIAL HISTORY

THE ANSONIA

A PICTORIAL HISTORY

THE ANSONIA

A PICTORIAL HISTORY

Southeast corner with surrounding buildings, circa 1905.

Photo of the southeast corner taken from street level, circa 1905.

A PICTORIAL HISTORY

This photo offers a rare view of the northeast corner of the Ansonia, circa 1905.

THE ANSONIA

Four

CONSTRUCTION

The south facade of the building during construction.

A PICTORIAL HISTORY

A view of the west side of the Ansonia during construction, taken from West 73rd Street.

THE ANSONIA

A view of the southeast side of the Ansonia during construction, up to the 12th floor, taken from the east side of Broadway and Amsterdam Ave.

A PICTORIAL HISTORY

38

This photo shows the Ansonia with exterior construction completed up to the corner towers.

THE ANSONIA

Light court on West 73rd Street during construction.

A PICTORIAL HISTORY

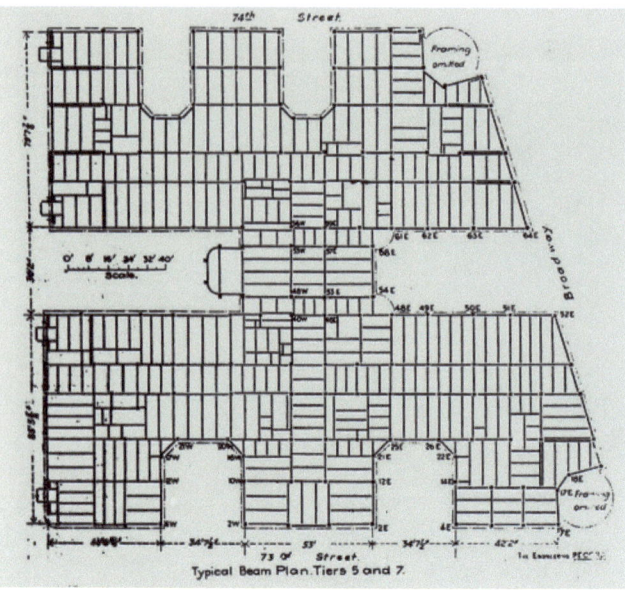

Floor beam plan.

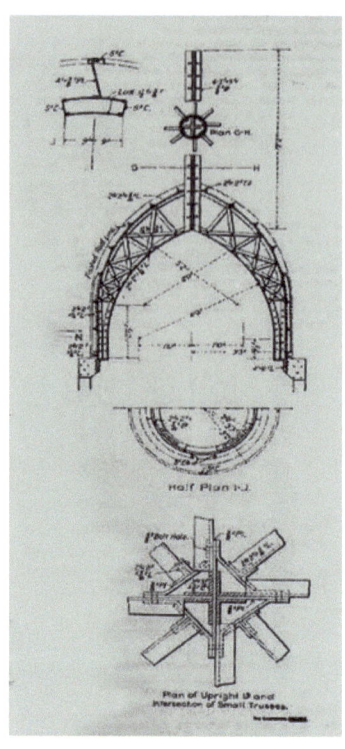

Tower steel section.

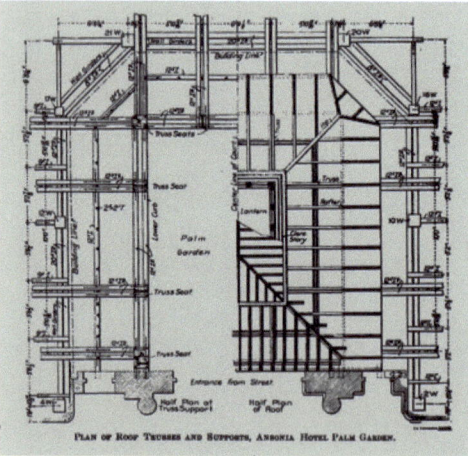

Plan of skylight roof trusses and supports.

Water supply system. When built, the buiding had 133 kitchens, with 133 sinks, laundry tubs and butler's pantry sinks, and 425 bathrooms with tubs, hand basins and about 550 water closet fixtures.

THE ANSONIA

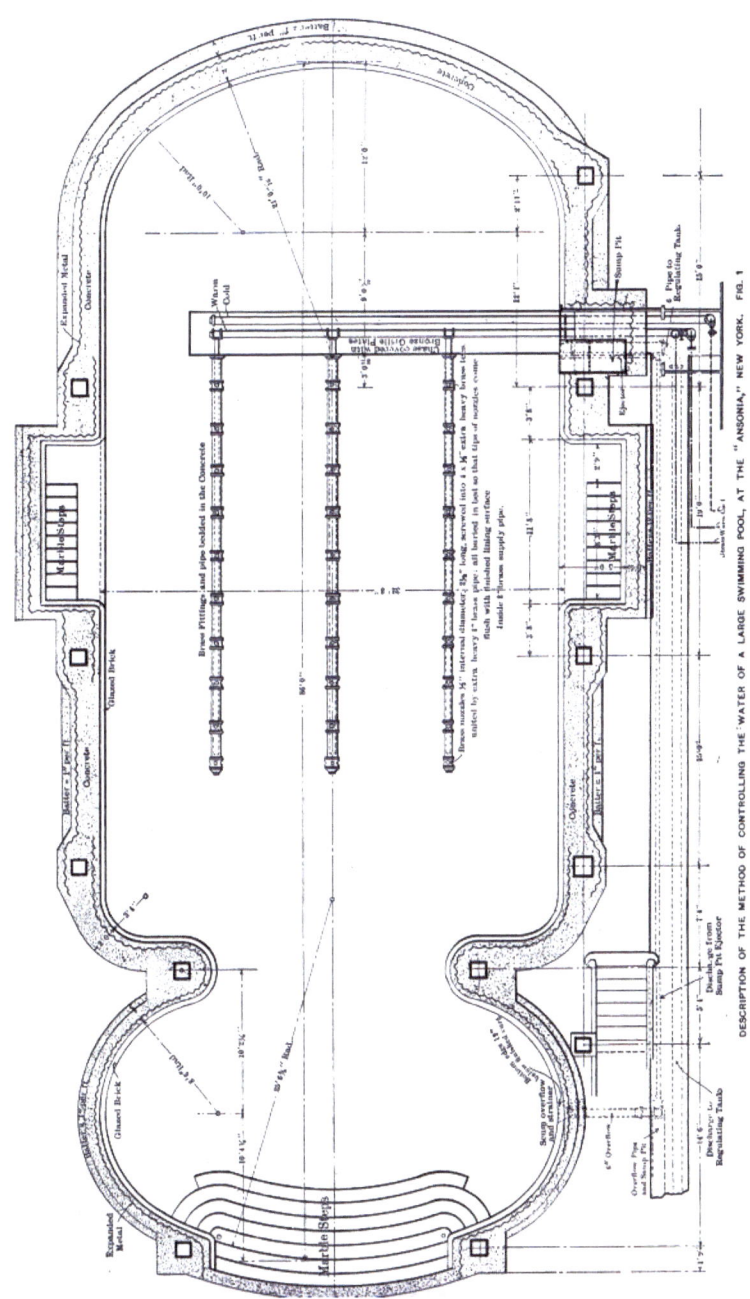

At the time it was built the Ansonia had the world's largest indoor swimming pool. It was located in the basement and was accessible to all guests.

A PICTORIAL HISTORY

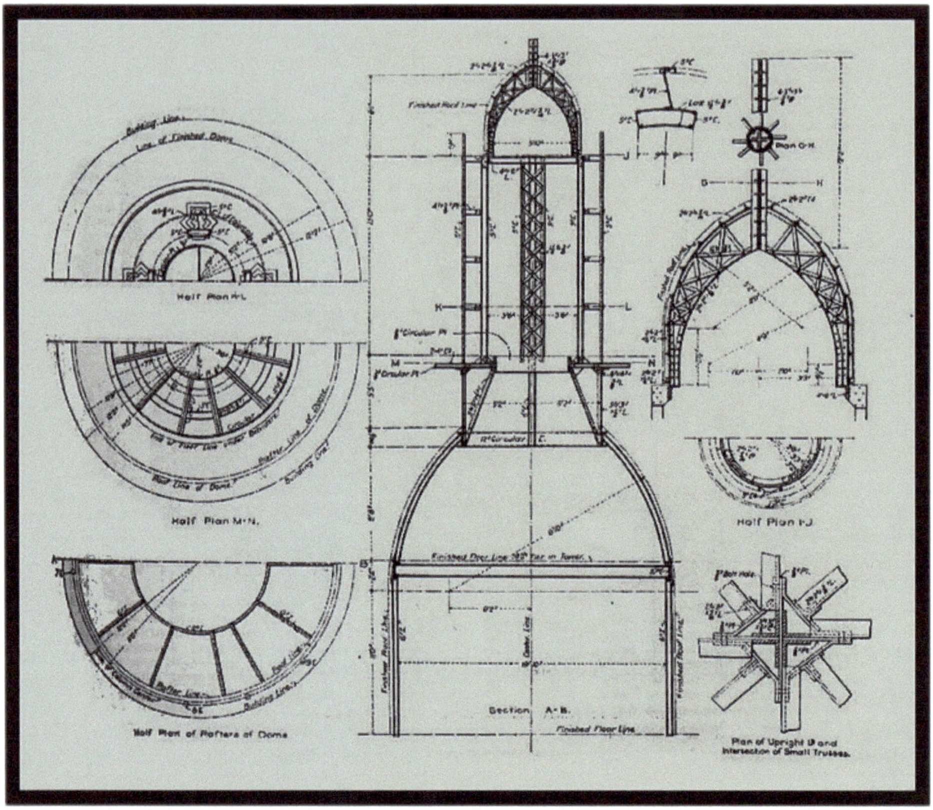

Steel Framework of Circular Corner Dome, Tower and Lantern.

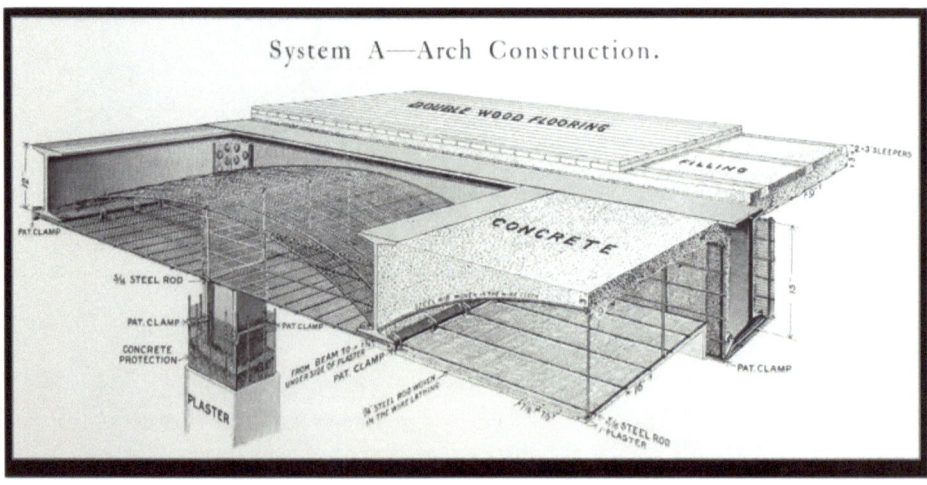

The Roebling System of Fire-Proof Construction.

THE ANSONIA

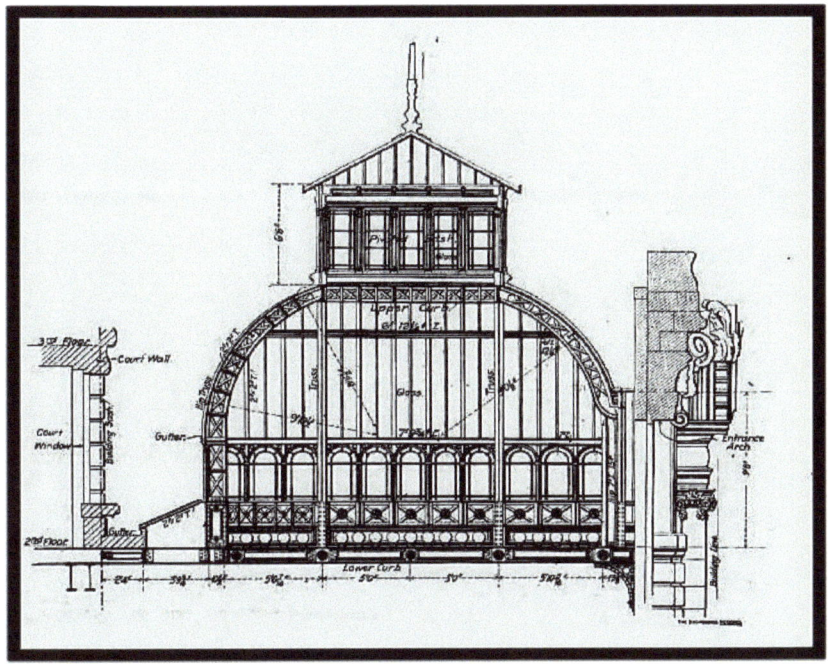

Glass and Steel Dome for Palm Garden and Grill Room.

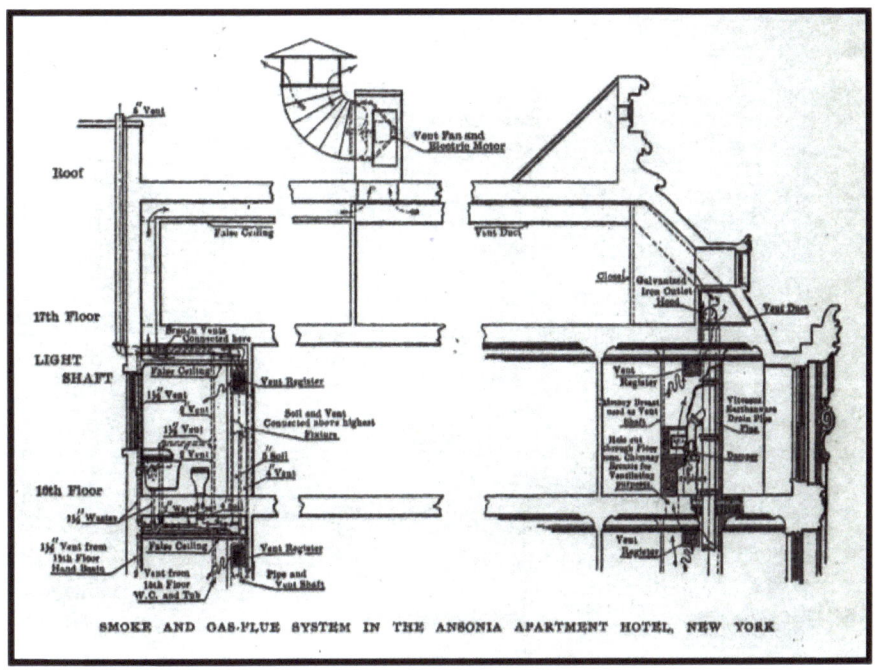

Original engineering illustrations for the flue system.

A PICTORIAL HISTORY

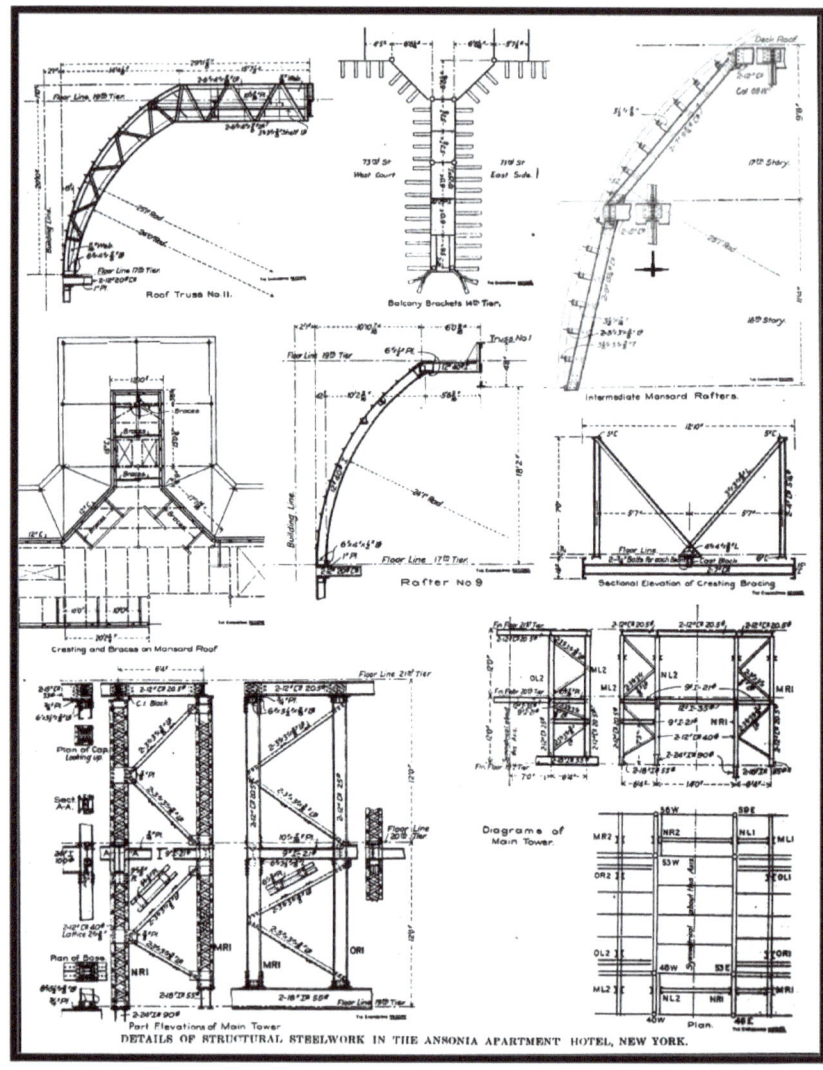

Original engineering illustrations of the Ansonia's mansard roof.

Five

VIEW FROM ROOF

The photograph for this souvenir postcard was taken from the roof of the Ansonia looking south. In the distance, from left to right, one can see St. Patrick's Cathedral, the Metropolitan Tower, the Times Building and the Singer Building. In the foreground, on the left, is the Dorilton.

A PICTORIAL HISTORY

Looking northward up Broadway.

Looking westward toward the Hudson River.

THE ANSONIA

Illustration of the northeast corner of the roof during construction.

A PICTORIAL HISTORY

This unique photo shows men preparing to lower one of the heavy ornamental cornices as part of a campaign to gather scrap metal for the WWII effort.

THE ANSONIA

Six
Floor Plans

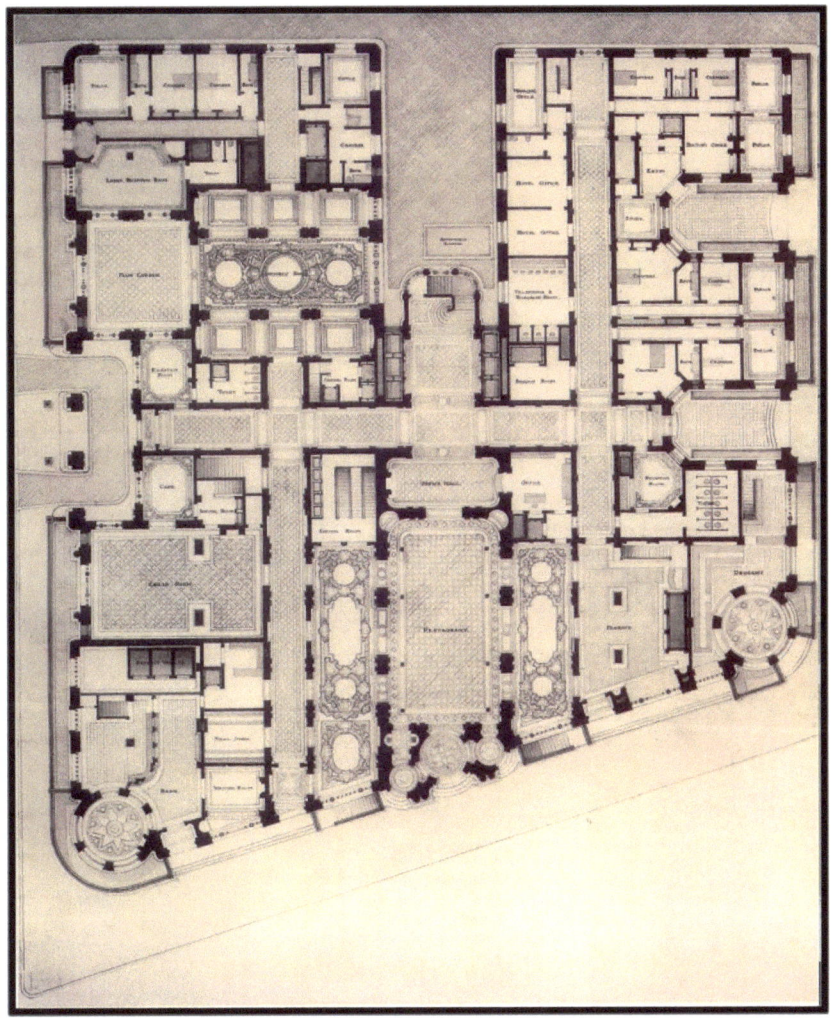

Original ground floor plan.

A PICTORIAL HISTORY

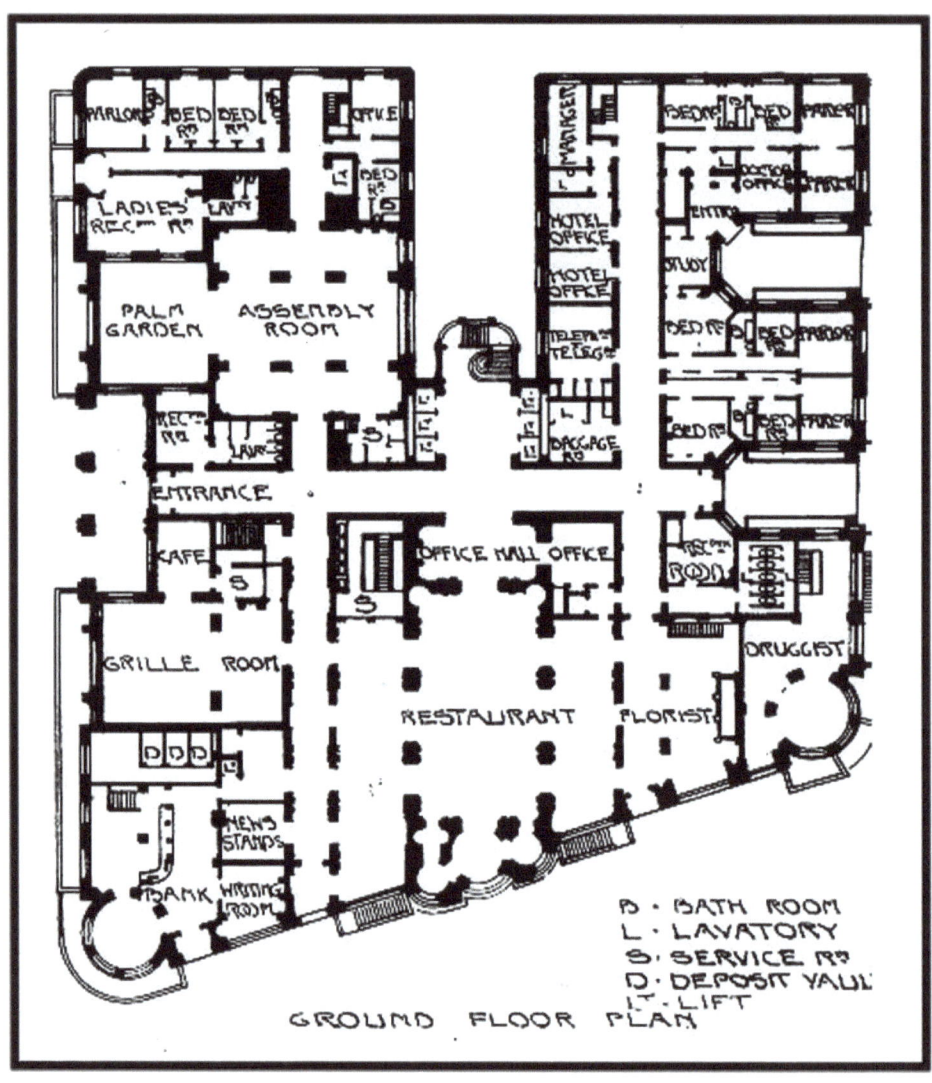

Ground floor plan, circa 1905.

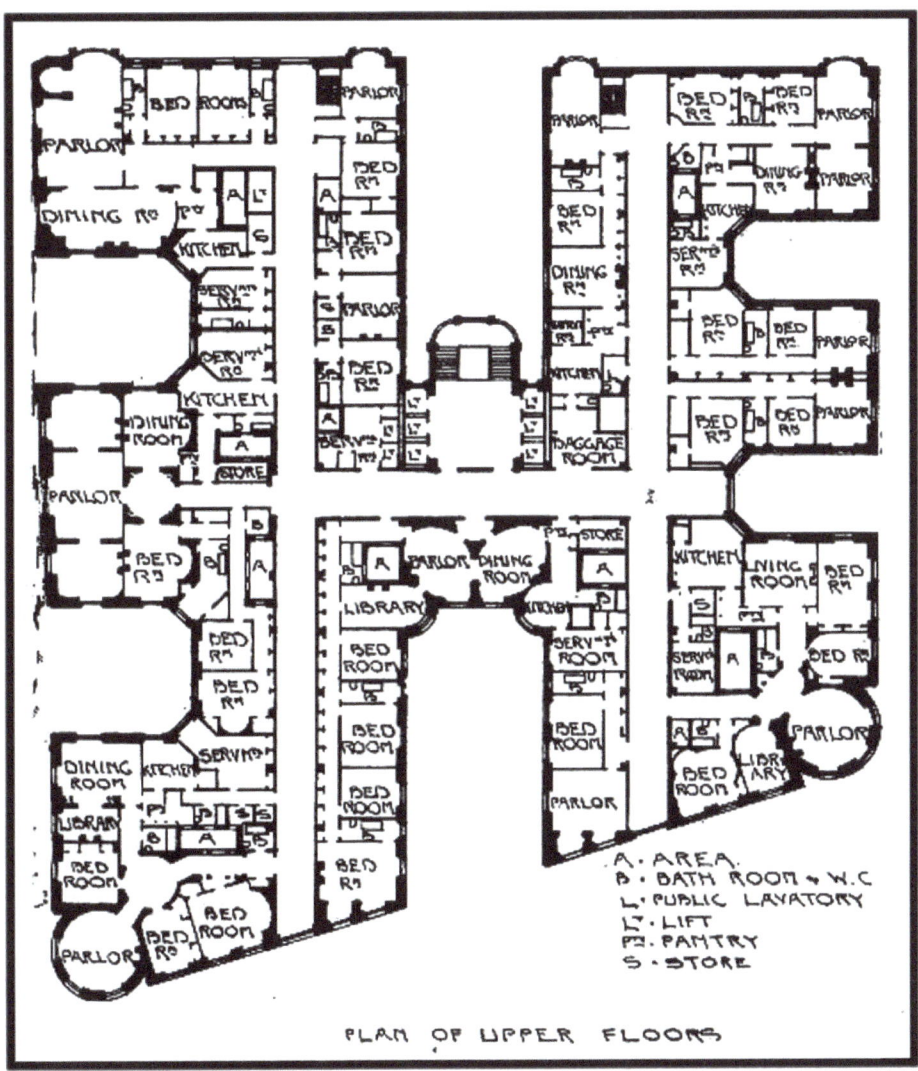

Upper floor plan, circa 1905.

A PICTORIAL HISTORY

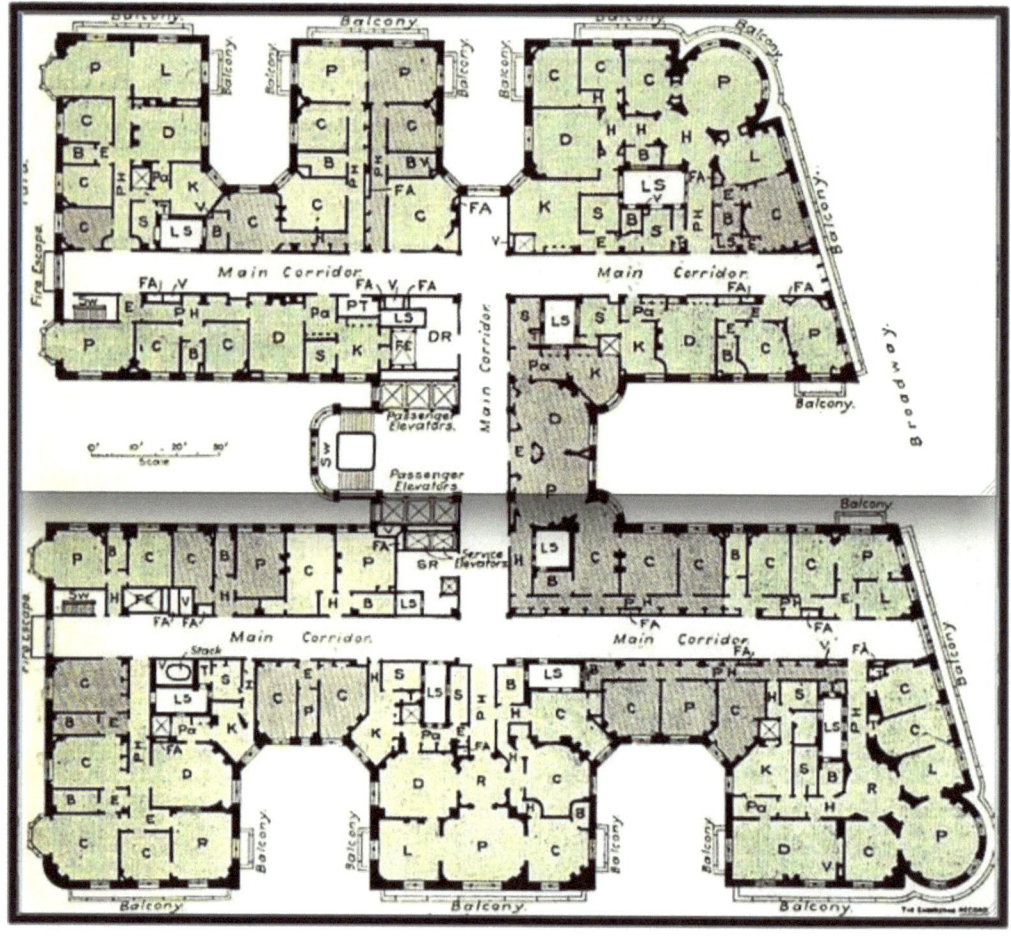

Typical floorplan of the Ansonia, circa 1907, as featured in the American Architect.

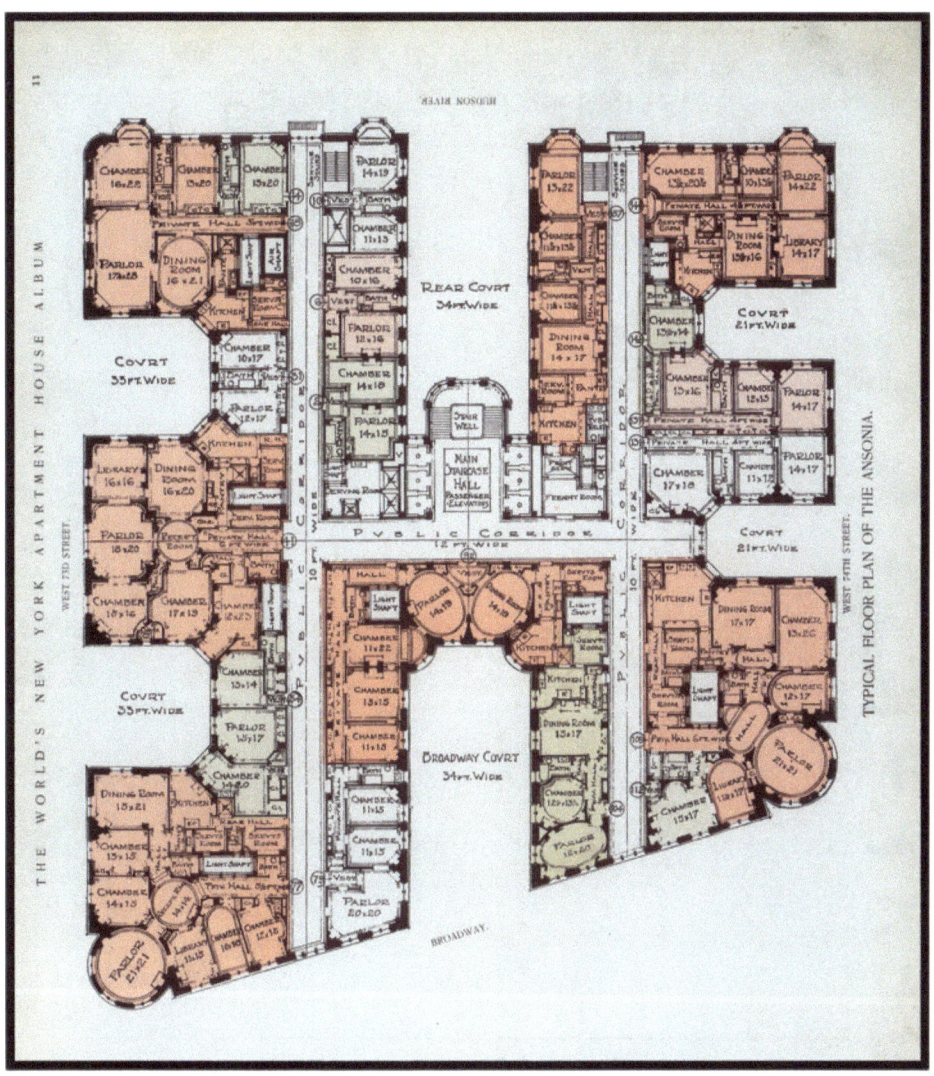

Typical floorplan of the Ansonia as featured in the 1910 edition of The World's Loose Leaf Album of Apartment Houses.

A PICTORIAL HISTORY

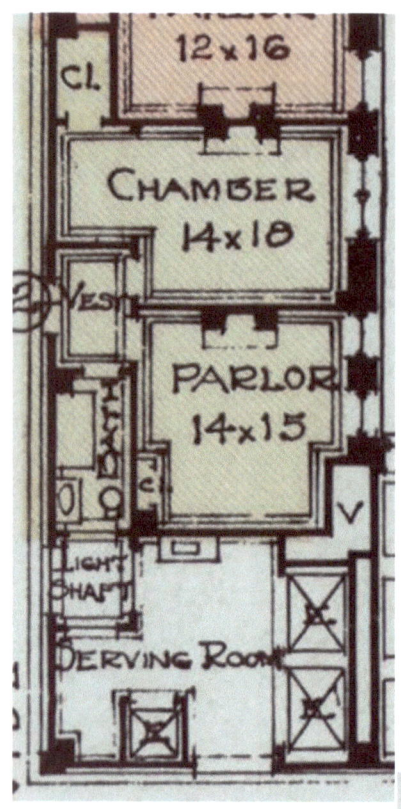

This floorplan shows a typical two-room apartment in the Ansonia. Entering through the vestibule foyer, the chamber on the left is a bedroom and includes a spacious closet. The Parlor overlooks the west light court and the curved window exterior of the grand staircase. During subsequent renovations, some apartments in this series annexed the former serving rooms to create a private kitchen.

Contemporary real estate agents have promoted the sale of apartments by shining a light on the Ansonia's social history, including the many luminaries who have resided there. Other selling points included the "quietude of 1 to 3 foot thick walls" and "grand circular living rooms."

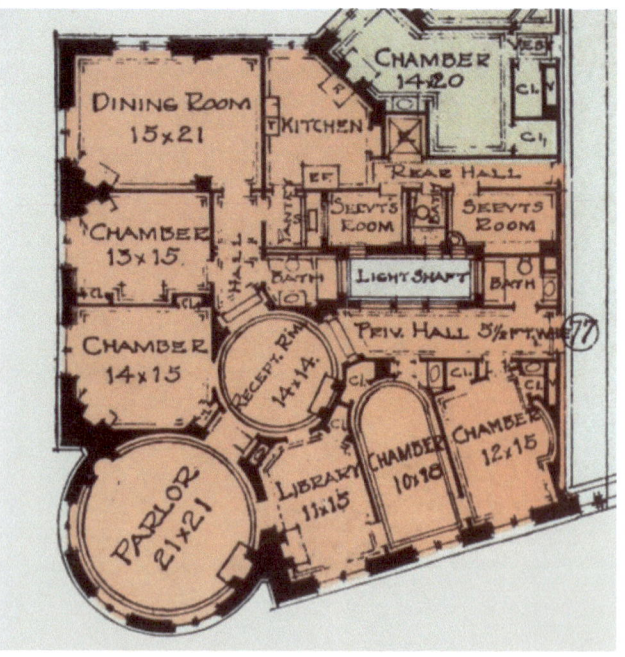

THE ANSONIA

Seven
Restaurants

A glimpse of the private dining room.

This photo was taken before guests arrived to enjoy a special dinner for the cast of the Wizard of Oz. The show opened in the Majestic Theatre on Broadway on January 21, 1903, where it ran for 293 performances until December 31, 1904.

The centerpieces are lifesize models of the Scarecrow and the Tin Woodman that were played by Fred Stone and David Montgomery. Ansonia resident Anna Fitziu played an assortment of roles in the chorus before moving to Paris to cultivate her opera career.

A PICTORIAL HISTORY

In addition to the public restaurants and cafes in the lobby, the Ansonia also offered a private dining room on the top floor of the building.

Another angle of the private restaurant on the top floor of the Ansonia.

A PICTORIAL HISTORY

60

The front and back of a vintage postcard with a photo and description of the interior of the English Grill Room.

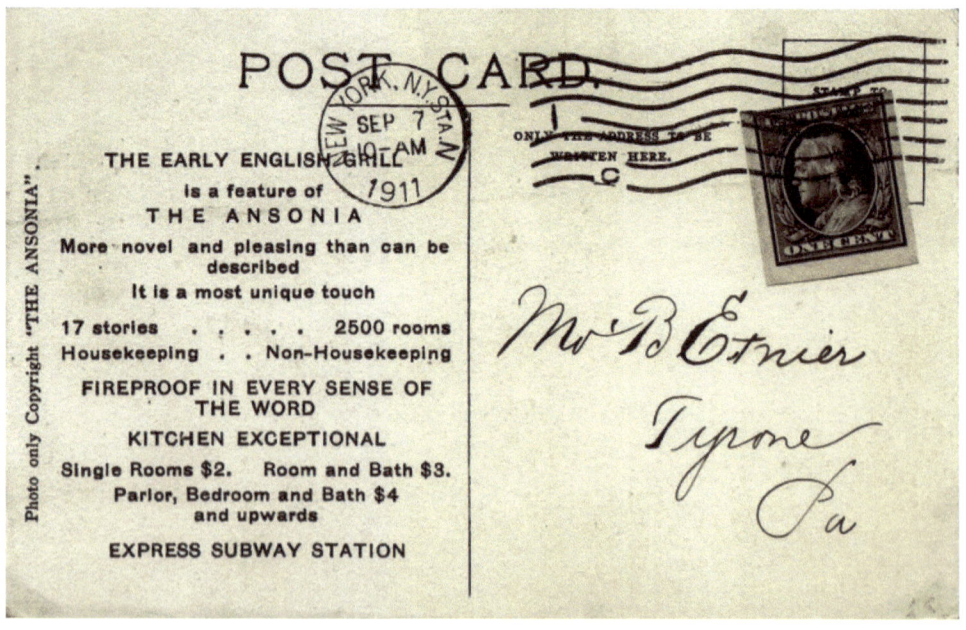

THE ANSONIA

The front and back of a vintage postcard with a photo and description of the mosaic fountain in the English Grill Room.

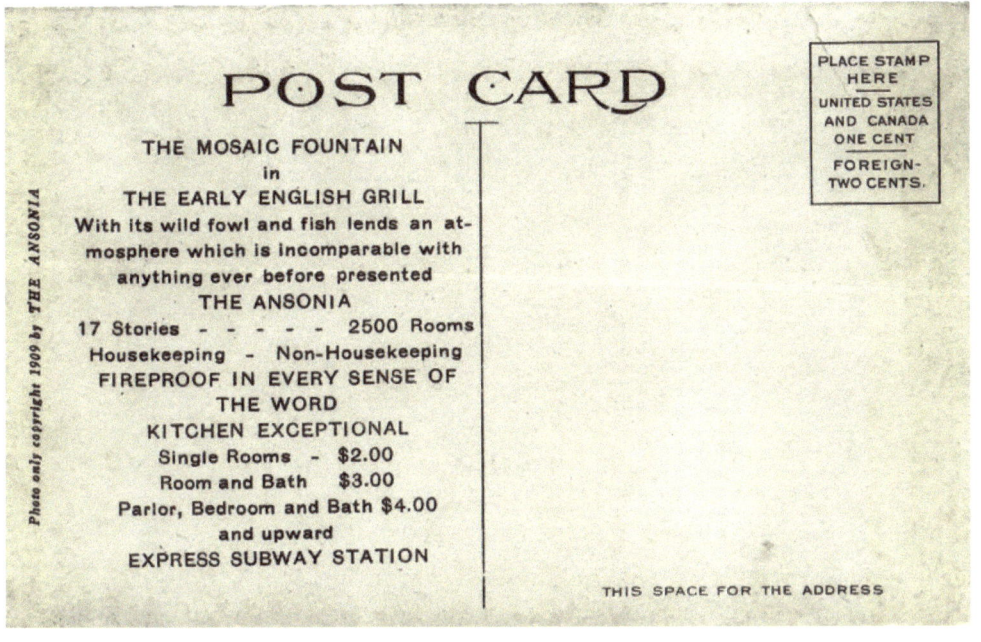

A PICTORIAL HISTORY

The above image of the English Grill Room was taken in 1919. It was alternatively known as "The Fountain Room" due to the elaborate fountain on the south side of the room.

Eight

Menus

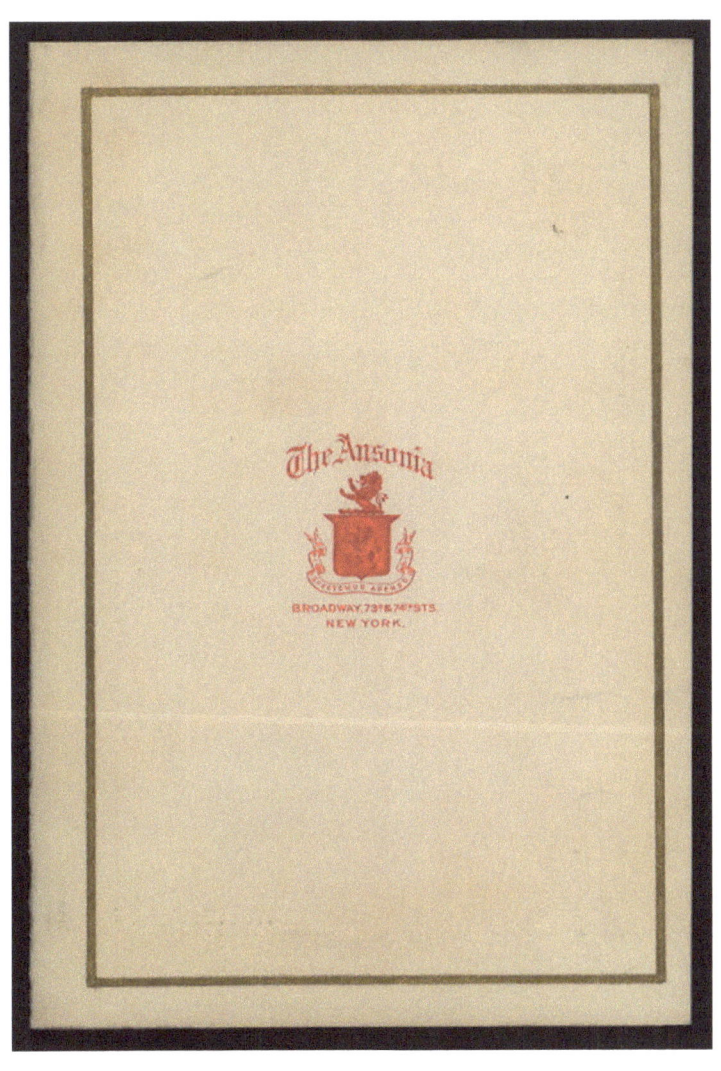

A PICTORIAL HISTORY

The Ansonia offered special menus on holidays.

This cover of the 1907 New Year's Eve menu presented the festive culinary selections within.

THE ANSONIA

This special menu was offered only on Thanksgiving. Some of the meals that were offered included: crab croquettes, sea bass a la Bourguignonne, broiled Spanish mackerel, oysters a la Villeroi, loin of beef à la de Lesseps, breast of partridge a la chasseur, English Snipe, Grouse, Ruddy, Woodcock and Golden Plover. Desserts included: green apple pie, Port wine jelly, cherry tarts, plum pudding and New England cider.

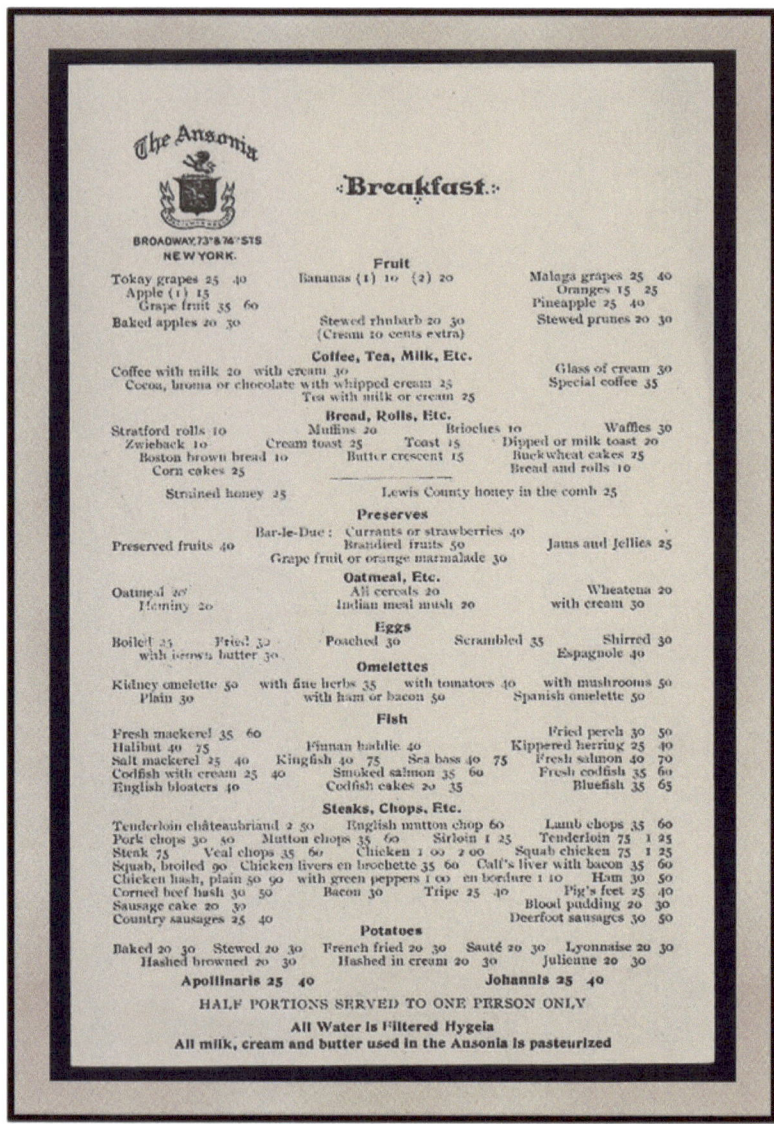

A Breakfast menu from the Ansonia, circa 1907. Guests could order a variety of egg dishes, including broiled, poached, scrambled, shirred and espagnole. Fish dishes that were offered included: mackerel, halibut, codfish, sea bass, salmon, perch and bluefish.

THE ANSONIA

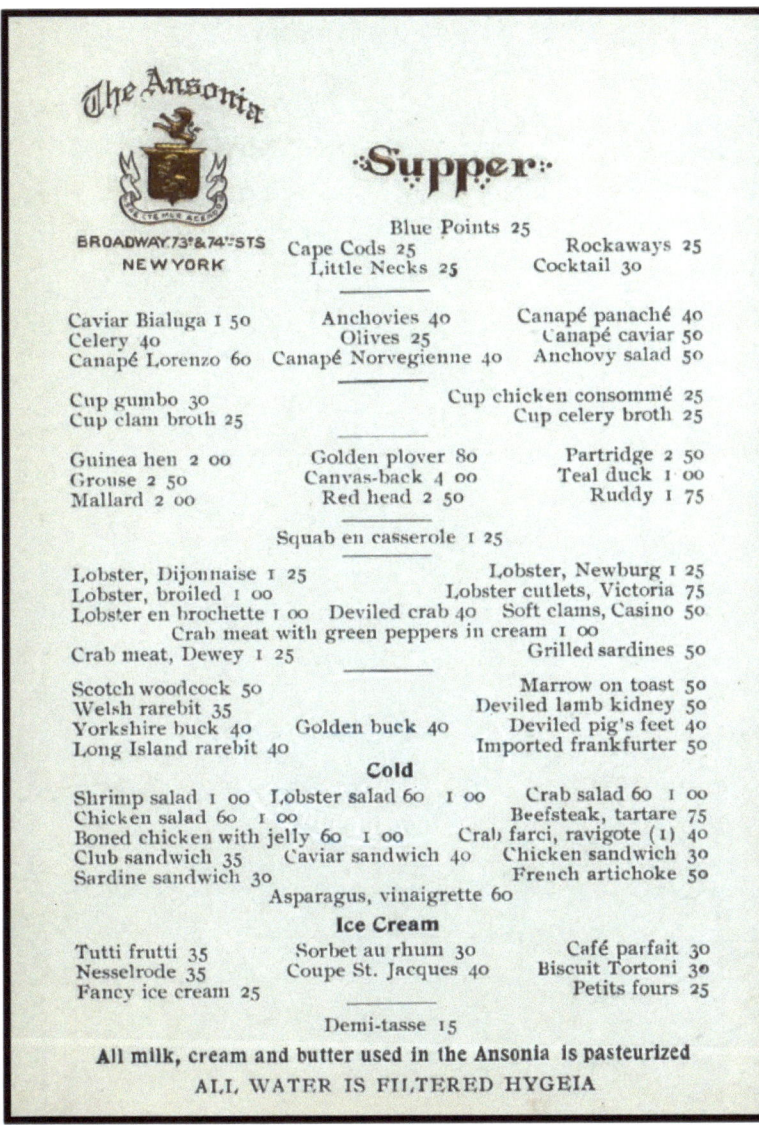

A Supper menu from the Ansonia, circa 1907. Some of the various lobster dishes included: Dijonnaise, broiled, en brochette, and as cutlets, with prices ranging from .75 - $1.25. Scotch woodcock, marrow on toast, deviled lamb kidney, deviled pig's feet, imported frankfurter, Welsh rarebit and Yorkshire buck were all available for 50 cents or less.

A PICTORIAL HISTORY

Roast

Capon . . . . . . half 2 00 whole 4 00		Beef	.40	70
Squab turkey 3 50		Mutton	.35	60
Turkey, giblet sauce. 50	90	Lamb	.45	80
Chicken 1 00	2 00			

Cold Dishes

Roast beef 40	70	Chicken 60	1 00	Squab		.90
Roast lamb 45	80	Turkey 60	1 00	Assorted cuts with		
Boned capon, jelly 60	1 00			chicken . .		.90

Game

Partridge	2 50	Mallard duck		2 00
Teal duck	1 00	Red-head duck		2 50
Grouse	2 50	Ruddy duck		1 75
Canvas-back duck	4 00	Squab guinea hen 1 00		2 00
Cold partridge	2 50	Quail		1 00

Vegetables

Potatoes,, boiled 15	25	French asparagus		1 25
Ansonia 20	30	Oyster Bay asparagus		.60
stuffed 20	35	French string beans		.40
French fried 20	30	French peas 25		40
German fried 20	30	Stuffed tomatoes 25		40
cream au gratin	30	Spinach 25		40
hashed in cream 20	30	Fresh artichokes		.50
Cauliflower	50	Fond d'artichauts, Dubarry . . .		.60
Beets	30	Stewed tomatoes		.25
String beans 30	50	Delmonte asparagus tips		.60

Salads

Lettuce and tomato 30	50	Lobster 60		1 00
Cucumber 25	40	Chicken 60		1 00
Watercress 25	40	Lettuce 25		40
Waldorf 30	50	Ansonia 30		50
Romaine 25	40	Louise, in pineapple		.75
Celery 25	40	Escarole 25		40
Chicory 25	40	Mayonnaise, extra		.10
Alligator pear	75			

Dessert

Wine jelly	.20	Baba au rhum	.30
Omelette soufflé	.60	Charlotte russe	.30
Omelette Surprise	.60	Assorted éclairs 15	25
Pie	.20	Petits fours	.20
Meringue Chantilly	.25	Caramel custard	.25

Ice Creams

Lemon ice 25	Coupe St. Jacques	.40
Vanilla 25	Nesselrode pudding	.35
Coffee 25	Roman punch	.30
Chocolate 25	Neapolitan	.30
Punch 30	Tutti frutti	.35

Fruits

Tokay grapes 25	40	Grape fruit 35		60
Malaga grapes 25	40	Pineapple 25		40
Plums 15	25	Oranges 15		25
Apples 15	25			

Coffee, Tea, etc.

Pot coffee 20	Lipton's Ceylon tea	.25
Chocolate 25	Japan tea	.25
Cocoa 25	Milk, per glass	.10
English breakfast tea 25	Cream, per glass	.25
Oolong tea 25	Pitcher cream	.10

Cheese

Philadelphia cream 15	25	Edam 15	25	Brie 20		30
Neufchâtel 15	25	Pineapple 15	25	American		.15
Roquefort 20	30	Camembert 15	25	Swiss 15		25
Canadian Imperial . .20		Port du Salut . . .15	25	Stilton 20		30
		Cheddar 20	30	Crackers		.10

HALF PORTIONS SERVED TO ONE PERSON ONLY
SPACIOUS BANQUET HALLS FOR WEDDINGS, PARTIES, ETC.

A la carte menu from the Ansonia, circa 1907. Guests could order partridge, duck, quail, turkey, chicken, beef, mutton and lamb. Desserts that were offered included: pie, Meringues Chantilly, Charlotte Russe, assorted éclairs and caramel custard.

THE ANSONIA

Nine
Lobby

A rare glimpse of the Ansonia's original lobby.

Original architectural elevation of the Ansonia's lobby.

THE ANSONIA

KEEN'S CHOP HOUSE
My God! Another Chop House?

Once upon a time, the Lambs gamboled where Keen's Chop House now stands, and playfully posted each other for dues that were overdue. And then, as the screen puts it, came the Talkies. Vaudeville languished; organizations supported by Vaudevillians shriveled; the Lambs' Club went places; and Keen's Chop House blossomed on the old site, giving America its meatiest mutton chops in the process.

Keen's, like many of the other chop houses, looks, smells, and feels like a very, very old English Inn. Its interior is old, smoky, and dim-lit—cleaner than the Cheshire Cheese, but not a whit less atmospheric.

And in keeping with its English traditions (maybe we didn't tell you that it has English traditions, but it has), the interior is hung with sporting prints, modern and not so modern, with etchings and water-colors of the Hunt, and with very old Playbills.

Here too, if you get your waiter in a talkative mood, he'll point out one of these old programs (playbills, to your English forebears)—a playbill of *Our American Cousin*, frayed now, and bloodstained; and he'll explain that here then is the playbill that Abraham Lincoln held in his hand the night of his assassination.

The waiters, too, are English, and an unwieldy sort of type; but they're willing, eager to please, and their accent reminds you of nothing so much as a steward on a British liner.

The fare is English, too—marvelous mixed grills, mutton chops pretty nearly as large as a boxing glove, though ever so much more tender, and the usual giant baked potatoes and good, rare roasts whose aroma is, taken all alone, sufficient as an appetizer.

The fare is satisfying, both as to quantity and quality; the prices fairly reasonable, considering; and the clientele, assorted. Around and about you, you'll find artists, actors, and plain, ordinary epicures—sportsmen of this day and of a day that has gone; prize-fighters, building up energy with the good food, and their hangers-on, watching them with awe and admiration. Here, in this erstwhile headquarters of New York's famous Dutch Treat Club, you'll find good food, a comfortable atmosphere, and plenty of leisure in which to enjoy both.

Off the ground floor lobby of the Ansonia space was rented to other businesses, including restaurants. Keen's Chop House was located in the Ansonia as early as 1903. In 1930 Willie Sutton, the bank robber, was arrested while having breakfast at Childs Restaurant in the Ansonia.

Ten

Assembly Room

To commemorate George Washington's birthday, the Ansonia's ballroom was decorated with American flags.

Photo of children attending a party in the Ansonia's Assembly Room to celebrate George Washington's birthday, circa 1910.

The view of the Ansonia's Assembly Room.

THE ANSONIA

Eleven

A Glimpse Inside

Vintage photo of a bed chamber in the Ansonia Hotel shows one of the six fireplaces in the entire suite. When the Ansonia hotel opened there were over five (5) dozen fireplaces on each floor.

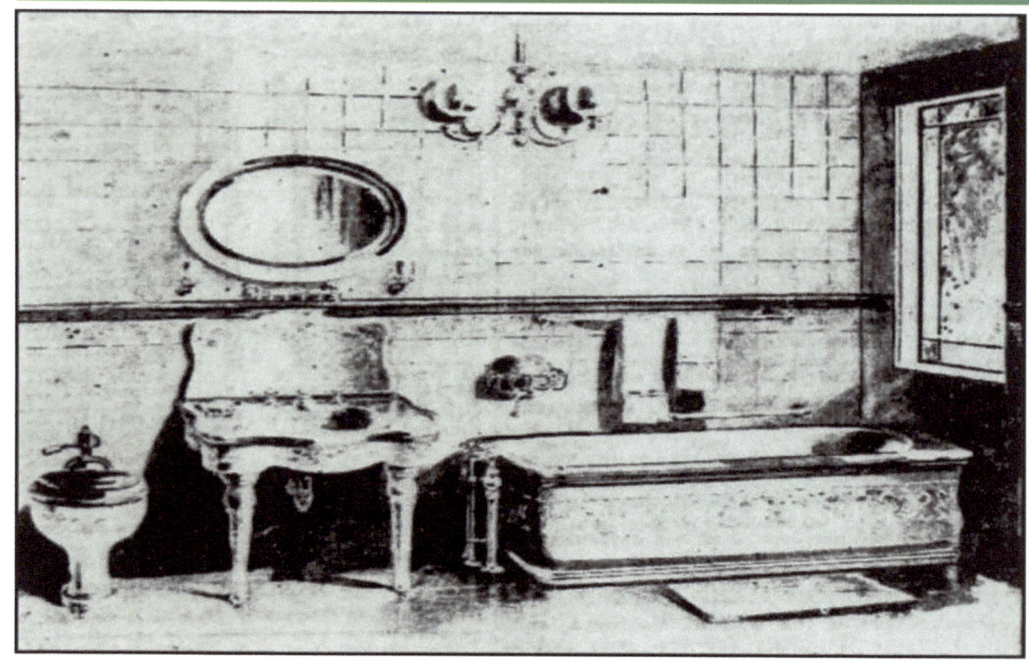

The sanitary appointments and the entire plumbing construction in the Ansonia Apartment Building have been executed by MILTON SCHNAIER & CO., contractors, No. 37 COLUMBUS AVE., BETWEEN 76TH and 77TH STS. The plumbing contract in the Ansonia Building is the largest that has ever been executed in the United States, and involves a cost exceeding $350,000.

The swimming pool has also been constructed by Milton Schnaier & Co. This pool will contain over 300,000 gallons of water. It is supplied with water from the Hudson River. Hot and cold salt water baths will be furnished as well as fresh water baths, and all of the water is filtered so as to make it perfectly clear. The water system for supplying water to the plumbing fixtures is an innovation, the like of which has never been attempted before. The plumbers have been at work in this building for the past two years, and the work has now reached a state of completion.

There are over 400 bathrooms, containing a solid porcelain bathtub, a solid porcelain wash basin and a solid porcelain toilet in each bathroom, and all are of the highest quality of material and workmanship; aside from these fixtures there are 600 additional toilets, 800 additional wash basins, the many appurtenances for the basement and kitchen, an ice water plant, engineer's room and the sixteenth floor kitchen and dining room. The plumbing contractors have also the contract for the dish washing machines. Installing two of Milton Schnaire's patent machines which will each have a capacity of washing and drying dishes in sixty seconds.

This is the only hotel in the world furnished with these dish washing machines, as they have only recently been patented by Mr. Schnaier. The plumbing in the Ansonia is the most elaborate, expensive and most complete ever undertaken in the construction of any building in the world.

- New York Daily Tribune, 1902.

THE ANSONIA

Twelve
W.E.D. Stokes

Photo of Stokes while at Yale, circa 1874.

W.E.D. Stokes, circa 1885.

A PICTORIAL HISTORY

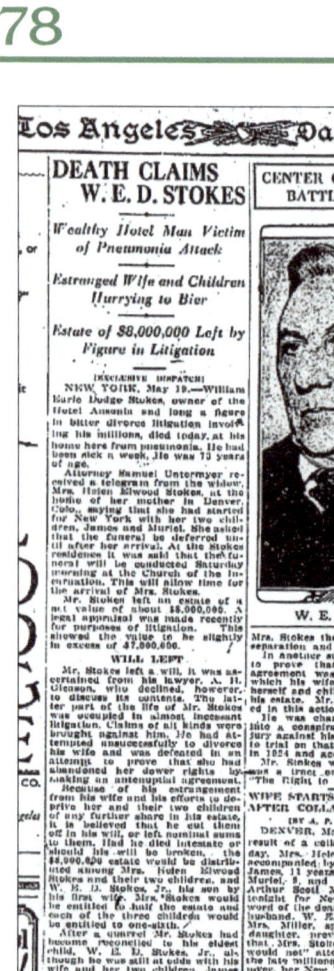

W.E.D. Stokes, circa 1896.

William Earle Dodge Stokes, the builder and owner of the Ansonia, and major developer of New York's Upper West Side, died on May 18, 1926. Though he was embroiled in numerous law suits at the time of his death, they were soon dismissed and his estate passed on to his eldest son. An agreement was soon made with Stokes' widow Helen Elwood, guardian of Stokes' children Helen and James who received $1.5 - $2 million. The agreement included awarding Ms. Elwood the principal of the $800,000 trust created by Stokes in an earlier litigation.

Thirteen

Residents

This above photo shows Babe Ruth having breakfast in his Ansonia apartment with boxer Jack Dempsey, circa 1927.

Babe Ruth
Baseball Outfielder and Pitcher.

A PICTORIAL HISTORY

The men in the above 1919 White Sox photo are:
FRONT ROW: Lynn, Risberg, Kerr, McClellan, Williams, Cicotte.
MIDDLE ROW: Schalk, Jenkins, Felsch, Gleason, E.Collins, J.Collins, Faber, Weaver.
BACK ROW: Shoeless Joe Jackson, Gandil, McMullin, Lowdermilk, James, Mayer, Murphy, Sullivan, Wilkinson.

    According to numerous accounts, in September, 1919, eight Chicago White Sox players met in first baseman Chick Gandil's Ansonia Hotel apartment and conspired to "throw" the 1919 World Series in which they were set to play against the Cincinnati Reds. In the most popular telling of the story, a group of gamblers including Arnold Rothstein provided the up-front cash.

    On October 1, 1919, the first game of the World Series, a public room in the Ansonia Hotel was set up with a large diamond-shaped chart on the wall where, as the action was telegraphed in, each play was read aloud and figures were moved around the chart's bases. Rothstein himself joined the hundreds gathered there, vicariously participating in the excitement. When he witnessed the prearranged signal that the series would be thrown, he walked out of the Ansonia's lobby.

    The White Sox lost. It has been said that the participating players earned $5,000 - $20,000 each. The eight baseball players, including the great "Shoeless" Joe Jackson, were acquitted by a grand jury for a lack of evidence. Despite the non-guilty verdict, they were banned from professional baseball for life.

Florenz Ziegfeld, Jr.
Broadway impresario.

Moss Hart
Playwright & theater director.

Elmer Rice
Playwright.

DeWolf Hopper
American actor, singer, comedian, and theatrical producer.

Cornell Woolrich
American novelist and short story writer.

A PICTORIAL HISTORY

Lillian Lorraine

American stage and screen actress of the 1910s and 1920s.

Sarah Bernhardt

French stage and early film actress.

Joan Bennett

American stage, film and television actress.

Dagmar Godowsky

Silent film actress.

Billie Burke

Broadway and film actress, best known as Glinda the Good Witch of the North.

Bidu Sayao

Brazilian opera soprano.

THE ANSONIA

Anna Held
Polish-born French stage performer and singer.

Bruna Castagna
Italian mezzo-soprano.

Tito Schipa
Italian tenore di grazia.

Antonio Scotti
Italian baritone.

Rose Levere
Lawyer and pastor of the First Spiritualist Church in New York.

A PICTORIAL HISTORY

Lily Pons

Operatic soprano and actress.

John F. Murtaugh

Playwright & theater director.

Abdu'l-Baha

The eldest son of Bahá'u'lláh, who became his father's successor as the head of the Bahá'í Faith.

Alessio De Paolis

Italian operatic tenor who specialized in character roles.

Jack Dempsey
World heavyweight boxing champion.

Fausto Cleva
Italian-born American operatic conductor.

Peter Doelger
Beer brewer.

Mischa Elman
Violinist.

A PICTORIAL HISTORY

Eleanor Steber
American operatic soprano.

Elisabeth Rethberg
German soprano.

Emmy Destinn
Czech operatic soprano.

Elisabeth Schwarzkopf
German-born Austrian/British soprano opera singer and recitalist.

THE ANSONIA

Estelle Taylor

Hollywood actress who was married to boxer Jack Dempsey.

Frances Alda

Operatic soprano.

Franco Corelli

Italian tenor.

Sergei Rachmaninoff

Russian composer, pianist, and conductor.

Enrico Caruso

Italian operatic tenor.

A PICTORIAL HISTORY

Friedrich Schorr

Austrian-Hungarian bass-baritone.

Geraldine Farrar

American soprano opera singer and film actress.

George Cehanovsky

Baritone and language coach.

Erika Morini

Austrian violinist who was considered to be the "most bewitching woman violinist of this century."

Karen Branzell

Swedish operatic contralto.

THE ANSONIA

Herbert Jansenn

German operatic baritone.

Feodor Chaliapin

Russian opera singer.

Jan Peerce

American operatic tenor.

Joan Sutherland

Australian dramatic coloratura soprano.

A PICTORIAL HISTORY

This photo shows actress Cleo Mayfield entering an automobile in front of the Ansonia in 1922 while she and her husband (Cecil Lean) were residents of the Ansonia Hotel.

Fourteen

VIEWS FROM BROADWAY

This photo was taken from Amsterdam Ave., north of 71st Street. The St. Andrew Hotel and the Ansonia Hotel are in the left background, circa 1905.

A PICTORIAL HISTORY

View of the Dorilton on the right and the Ansonia in the distance on the left, circa 1910.

The Ansonia can be seen on the left side background of this vintage photo.

A PICTORIAL HISTORY

View of the Ansonia & the Colonial Club from the East side of Amsterdam Avenue.

A sketch of the Colonial Club from the New York Tribune.

THE ANSONIA

The Ansonia can be seen in the distance of this photo while Broadway was being paved.

A PICTORIAL HISTORY

Restoration of Broadway on the east side of the Ansonia following the construction of the Subway.

THE ANSONIA

A PICTORIAL HISTORY

W.E.D. Stokes, circa 1917.

www.ingramcontent.com/pod-product-compliance
Lightning Source LLC
Chambersburg PA
CBHW042325150426
43192CB00004B/123